The Sacredness of the Sacred Heart

By

Joseph Livingston

Foreword

This book, *The Sacredness Of The Sacred Heart,* is a follow-up of my previous book called, *You Are Mine Now.*

Without doubt, the loving help of Ellen and James Hrkach has contributed to these two books.

I am a Catholic Christian evangelist who travels the world promoting and speaking about Christianity and, in particular, Jesus and Mary.

The popularity of the book, *You Are Mine Now,* which just seems to fly off the shelves – in particular at my conferences – is a testimony to the editing and digital skills of Ellen and James.

I am deeply indebted to this Catholic couple, who are a shining example of loving Christianity.

May the Good Lord continue to bless their marriage and publishing exploits.

With all my love…

Chapter 1
Eternity in Milliseconds

Whenever anyone thinks of anything that is sacred, it can mean different things to different people.

For instance, "Oh, you can't go there or walk there, for it is sacred ground." The North American Indians treated their burial grounds as holy and exclusive. It is a great mistake to enter these particular burial grounds without being warned as to the very sacredness of the Indians' ancestral resting places.

We, too, have our cemeteries, which by and large are treated with respect.

Is it spiritual?

Is it respect for our dead loved ones?

Do we miss their presence in our hearts and our lives?

There are so many questions to answer.

The physical and emotional jolt of losing a loved one can be devastating.

Sacredness is eternal.

Jesus is eternal.

Is it a footstep beyond the realm of normality to be able to actually touch sacredness?

The woman in the Gospel who suffered from terrible bleeding, she touched sacredness (Mark 5: 21-34). She knew that if she could only touch the garment of Jesus, she would be healed.

This spiritual experiment that we have stumbled upon was two-fold.

Firstly, at the very moment the woman had touched Jesus's garment, he knew that power had gone out of him.

What we don't know is; did the reduction in power within Jesus last only a millisecond?

It seems intriguing, doesn't it?

Eternity means eternity, therefore eternity cannot be reduced to or even contained for more than a millisecond.

Therefore, it seems logical to assume that the sacred power of Jesus was immediately restored by some form of supernatural dynamo.

The second part of the two-fold question is this: When Jesus exclaims, "Who touched me?" the apostles immediately reply, "But, Master, everybody's touching you."

From this perspective, we see the human response to the eternal power of sacredness – misunderstanding.

The apostles tended to misunderstand the symmetry of Jesus's supernatural logic.

When we read the gospels with human eyes and understanding we fail to comprehend the enormity of sacredness.

But through the discipline of prayer, deep-felt prayer, the veil begins to be removed, and we begin to see difficult situations with a soothing clarity.

Chapter 2
Loving Surrender

The veil of our human understanding is not easy to remove.

If we introduce love – true love – our spiritual blindness becomes less blurred, especially when it's a love of prayer.

Love with all its components is enhanced when a degree of surrender is added to the recipe.

Surrender, in effect, becomes the yeast.

Without surrender, especially in loving prayer, there is no real or true success.

Peace, too, will thrive with a mutual respect and surrender of entrenched ideologies.

Nothing in this world comes to fruition without heartfelt and soul-searching actions.

Throughout this willingness to surrender, our souls become aligned with the sacredness of Jesus's Heart in a sort of spiritual osmosis.

However, we must be willing to surrender everything to Jesus. And, we can only truly experience the supernatural benefits of surrender by praying for this wonderful grace.

When we realise that a complicated situation has arisen, especially when we or others experience ill health, the only solution is to surrender everything to Our Saviour Jesus.

Divine Mercy will then flow automatically towards us like a river of light.

Mercy is unstoppable when there are no barriers of self to block the flowing current of grace.

Of course, throughout this surrender, we can ask Jesus to heal us too.

Just like the woman who touched His garment, her healing took place because she totally surrendered to the magnificent supernatural power of Jesus.

She already knew beforehand that something miraculous would happen. Maybe throughout the years of her terrible illness, she became totally disillusioned by the fruitless attempts of various doctors to help her.

Therefore, something happened to her mental state.

Something was revealed to her by divine providence.

I believe she totally surrendered to the Messiah.

She knew in a sort of a way that this was the real deal. That this was the moment her torment would end.

She was rewarded.

Oh, to have been there!

To have actually witnessed this miracle.

The woman would have been ecstatic, running around in a haze of happiness, relief, and total peace.

Her outstanding faith intermingled with the total surrender ensured that there could only be one end result.

This is only *one* example from the gospels for us to cling to (Mark 5:21).

Matthew, Mark, and Luke all tell this story.

They make sure the reader identifies with the blessing and help that Our Lord and Saviour will bring to those who *truly* believe.

Chapter 3
Saint Margaret Mary Alacoque

Saint Margaret Mary Alacoque, was born on the 22nd July 1647 in a place called Le Hautecour in the Duchy of Burgundy, France.

She was the only daughter of Claude and Philiberte Lamyn Alacoque, who also had several sons.

From an early childhood, Margaret was described as showing intense love for the Blessed Sacrament.

She also preferred silence and prayer to childhood play.

After her First Communion at the age of nine, she practised in secret severe corporal mortification until rheumatic fever confined her to bed for four years.

At the end of this period, having made a vow to the Blessed Virgin to consecrate herself to religious life, she was instantly restored to perfect health.

In recognition of this favour, she added the name Mary to her baptismal name of Margaret.

According to later accounts of her life, she had visions of Jesus Christ, which she thought were a normal part of human experience and continued to practice austerity.

Her family was plunged into poverty after her father died, when a family relative refused to hand over the assets of the Alacoque family.

During this traumatic time, Margaret made frequent visits to pray before the Blessed Sacrament in the local church.

However, when she was seventeen, the family regained their fortune and her mother encouraged her to socialise, in the hope of her finding a suitable husband.

Out of obedience, and believing that her childhood vow was no longer binding, she began to accompany her brothers to social events, attending dances and balls.

One night after returning home from a carnival dressed in her finery, she experienced a vision of Christ scourged and bloodied.

Christ reproached her for her forgetfulness of Him; yet He also reassured her by demonstrating that His Heart was filled with love for her, because of the childhood promise that she had made to His Blessed Mother.

As a result, she determined to fulfil her vow and entered – when almost 24 years of age – The Visitation Convent at Paray Le Monial on the 25th May 1671, intending to become a nun.

Margaret Mary was subjected to many trials to prove the genuineness of her vocation. She was admitted to wearing the religious habit on the 25th August 1671, but she was not allowed to make her religious profession on the same date of the following year, which would have been normal.

A fellow novice described Margaret Mary as being humble, simple, and frank, but above all, kind and patient.

Finally, she was admitted to profession on the 6th of November 1672. It is said she was assigned to the infirmary and was not very skilful at her tasks.

Margaret Mary was steadfast in her vocation and worked hard to prove the validity of the visions that she received about the Sacred Heart.

She was initially rebuffed by her mother superior and was unable to convince theologians about the truth of the visions.

A noted exception was the Jesuit Saint Claude de la Colombiere, who supported her.

The devotion to The Sacred Heart was officially recognised 75 years after the death of Saint Margaret Mary.

In his encyclical *Miserentissimus Redemptor*, Pope Pius X1 stated that Jesus Christ had "manifested Himself" to Saint Margaret and referred to the conversation between Jesus and Saint Margaret several times.

St. Margaret Mary Alacoque

Chapter 4
Visions

In the monastery, Saint Margaret Mary received several private revelations of The Sacred Heart, the first on the 27th December 1673 and the final one, 18 months later.

The visions revealed to her the form of the devotion, the chief features being the reception of Holy Communion on the First Friday of each month, Eucharistic Adoration during a Holy Hour on Thursdays, and the celebration of the Feast of The Sacred Heart.

She stated that in her vision she was instructed to spend an hour every Thursday night to meditate on Jesus's Agony in the Garden of Gethsemane.

The Holy Hour practice later became widespread among Catholics.

On the 27th December 1673, the feast of Saint John, Margaret Mary reported that Jesus permitted her to rest her head upon His Heart, and then disclosed to her the wonders of His love.

Telling her that He desired to make them known to all mankind and to diffuse the treasures of His goodness, and that he had chosen her for this work.

Initially discouraged in her efforts to follow the instruction she had received in her visions, Margaret Mary was eventually able to convince her superior, Mother De Saumaise, of the authenticity of her visions.

However, she was unable to convince a group of theologians of the validity of her apparitions, nor was she any more successful with many of the members of her own community. She suffered greatly at their hands.

Eventually she received the support of Saint Claude de la Colombière S.J. the community's confessor for a time who declared that the visions were genuine.

In 1683, opposition in the community ended when Mother Merlin was elected Superior and named Margaret Mary as her assistant. She later became Novice Mistress, and saw the Monastery observe the Feast of The Sacred Heart privately, beginning in 1686.

Two years later, a chapel was built at Paray Le Monial to honour The Sacred Heart.

Saint Margaret Mary Alacoque died on 17th October 1690.

Chapter 6
Veneration

After Saint Margaret Mary died, the devotion to the Sacred Heart was fostered by the Jesuits. The practice was not officially recognised until 75 years later.

The discussion of Saint Margaret Mary's own mission and qualities continued for years. All her actions, her revelations, her spiritual maxims, her teachings regarding the devotion to The Sacred Heart – of which she was the chief exponent – were subjected to the most severe and minute examination.

Finally, the Sacred Congregation of Rites passed a favourable note on the heroic virtues of this "Servant of God."

In March 1824, Pope Leo X11 pronounced her Venerable and on 18th of September 1864 Pope Pius 1X, declared her Blessed.

When her tomb was canonically opened in July 1830, two instantaneous cures were recorded.

Her incorrupt body rests above the side altar in the Chapel of the Apparitions, located at the Visitation Monastery in Paray Le Monial, and many striking blessings have been claimed by pilgrims attracted there from all parts of the world.

Saint Margaret Mary Alacoque was canonised by Pope Benedict XV in 1920, and in 1929 her liturgical commemoration was included in the General Roman Calendar for celebration on 17th of October, the day of her death. In the reforms of 1969, the feast day was moved to the prior day 16th of October.

"Most Sacred Heart of Jesus, I place all my trust in You"

Chapter 7
Openness

If we act and speak in openness, there is an obvious ray or aura of integrity that seems to exude to the other person or crowd who happens to be listening to what is being said.

Openness of heart is a grace from God.

If someone speaks with a seemingly disguised sense of purpose, it can often be detected by the true listening heart. Therefore, when we speak in love and power, the Heart seems to guide our whole communication process.

If we think of Jesus's Sacred Heart, it makes good common sense to realise that when Our Saviour spoke, He really did get to the heart of the matter!

A Sacred Heart was pulsating with Divinity. Each Sacred Heartbeat became like a missile of loving penetration.

Most people in Jesus's time realised that He was different. He spoke with authority, and this sometimes got up the noses of those *in* authority.

But, there was no denying that he was *different*. Especially when his Sacred Heart began to melt the hearts of those who listened to his loving and powerful words.

I have often wondered what it would have been like on that mountainside when Our Saviour spoke the famous words of the beatitudes.

Let's just take one of the beatitudes;

"Blessed are the Peacemakers for they shall be called...Sons of God."

How immense and effective are these glorious words...whenever there is an argument in your family.

Whenever there is discord in government.

Whenever war erupts and nation fights against nation.

Whenever true love is scorned.

Whenever babies are aborted.

The list is endless. Whenever we try to bring peace and at least try to resolve the above-mentioned situations, something truly remarkable happens.

It is almost like an electrical connecting wire pulsates between Jesus's Sacred Heart and our own weak heart.

This electrical charge seems to transfer a pulsating desire to help Our Saviour. Our hearts actually become like a dynamo continually recharging at each enormous heartbeat of Jesus.

Can the heart of Jesus actually beat within our own heart?

Truly, I believe it can and it does.

How often has our heart melted at the sight of a baby in distress? Or the death of a close relative?

Atheists will say these types of emotions are human nature in operation. I disagree with that assumption.

Whenever we feel that emotion bursting through, Jesus's Sacred Heart (within) is actually melting our hearts with His sacred compassion, warmth and love.

I remember a funeral for a good friend of mine. At that time, I was part of The Legion of Mary. I asked Our Lord to let HIS emotion flow through me at the funeral service.

Well, Our Lord didn't miss me and hit the wall!

I cried like a baby at the end.

Let's analyse what happened in this situation.

First of all, I believed that Jesus WOULD flow through me.

Secondly, I was open to His Divine Will.

Thirdly, it proved to me that Jesus IS in our hearts.

Jesus actually proved without a doubt that His all-powerful Sacred Heart can overcome anything in our lives. Even down to affecting our emotions and thought processes.

But we *must* surrender to Him.

That way, Jesus will flow through us like a river of light.

Chapter 8
The Human Heart

It is within each and every person to achieve a small, local, and manageable change and it starts in the heart.

To change for the better seems to be the socially acceptable thing to do.

The human heart is relatively small in size, yet it is the most powerful and dynamic organ in the body. It is a source of life and this life gushes and pulsates to all areas of the human anatomy, and from there it can open up to the whole world.

How do we achieve change in the world?

Firstly, we must act locally, and this begins with ourselves. There is no point in us trying to solve the terrible problems in the world if we do not have peace in our own hearts in the first place.

Every political statement, every word of legislation, every directive is truly meaningless, unless we implement these actions with the motive of peace in our hearts.

The heart sends out vital signals to the other parts of the body and even to other people.

The meaning of some simple phrases that are used in everyday life can be very effective. For instance, "we had a good heart-to-heart chat last night" or "my heart went out to so and so," and "let's get to the heart of the matter."

All these sayings emanate social concern and well-being towards others and are the true essence of social power.

We will never change even the smallest issue, if it is not in peoples' hearts in the first place.

The heart transcends all cultures and belief systems.

Is the human heart sacred? Or is it to be treated with irreverence. Can it be a battlefield of bitterness or a cradle of comfort?

Can we control these feelings and emotions? I think we can. If we take the comparison of the human heart as a pastoral cycle, for instance. The experiences that we feel can be subjected to social analysis.

This automatically leads us to reflection both in a systematic and spiritual sense. This results in a greater understanding and celebration of God's life within us.

The shalom of our very being is responsive to external forces. For instance, the world we live in is topsy turvy. We never take time to sit in silence. Do we ever go out into nature and see God's creation, or listen to a soothing piece of music or even reflect in meditative prayer? All these actions induce tranquillity.

But cut off from this food of peace, the heart will function irregularly both in the physical and emotional sense.

Branching out from the heart are the arteries. The arteries

carry the pumped blood to the extremities of the human body.

If we take the analogy of a physically and emotionally healthy heart pouring life to the rest of the body in an unrestricted way, we do live life to the fullest. If the arterial lifeline is 'blocked' in any way, problems (even death) ensue.

A heart without truth and love will never understand the essence of civilisation and will always be retarded in growth, continually contributing to the whirlwind of social disintegration.

A true heart of peace will accept the kinship of all creatures and acknowledge unity with the universe.

Chapter 9
The Arterial Lifeline

As previously mentioned, if the lifeline of the arteries is blocked, death can ensue.

The heart is a pump that pulsates every second of our existence.

Let's imagine the arteries as some form of conduit.

These conduits carry the blood to all areas of the body.

The Sacred Heart of Jesus carries light and grace not only to the extremities of our human body, but if accepted properly the wonderful graces of Jesus's heart, we can extend to the whole world.

Acceptance is the key. We must accept that Jesus's Sacred Heart actually resides in our own hearts.

That is why the Sacred Lifeline is so important. If we consecrate ourselves to the Sacred Heart of Jesus, it allows the Divinity of Christ to permeate our heart with a love that can only be produced by Jesus Himself.

Therefore, if we are conscious of this important fact, it allows us to spread the love of Jesus easily.

Sometimes in our often-chaotic lifestyles, we open our

mouths before engaging the brain.

I would like to take this reality a bit further.

How many times throughout our lives do we feel something in our heart that is loving and sincere, and yet we can eventually shrug this feeling off and launch into a verbal betrayal of these heartfelt feelings?

We can then analyse these unkind words and think, "Why the heck did I say that?"

It's ultimately a matter of patience or trying to cultivate this great attribute.

They say patience is a virtue. It certainly is, especially when we realise we have just destroyed somebody's character using one of the most important human organs, the tongue.

Our human organ, the tongue, can bring untold happiness to other people in our lives. But the tongue can also be used to bring destruction and untold grief to those people around us.

Invariably, when an argument increases, it can lead to violence.

This eventuality of violence is actually a desecration of the Sacred Heart of Jesus within us.

Unknowingly, this can happen a lot more often than people would care to realise.

Violence does not always mean physical violence. The violence within our souls towards another human being is actually a bigger scar.

Each human soul is scarred through sin. This is an undeniable fact. So, we should take great care when dealing with others in the ups and downs of everyday life.

Can the scars in our soul affect the heart?

The soul is God.

It is a gift from God alone.

God is spirit, therefore when we sin, the scars in our soul must be able to link up to the heart, because both are gifts from God and a source of undeniable sacredness.

Our hearts can feel downcast after an argument especially when we realise that it was our very own fault.

This downcast feeling is the eternal soul of God within us sending a signal grace to our heart.

Yes, it is very uncomfortable to realise that we are in the wrong in certain situations.

That's why it is so important to visit the sacrament of reconciliation frequently.

Jesus's presence within the confessional is undeniable.

At the moment of absolution, not only do we receive a mini-exorcism, but it is actually Jesus blessing us with His unfathomable compassion through the priest *in Persona Christi (in the person of Christ)*.

This spiritual miracle is often overlooked by the laity.

It seems very obvious that the supernatural events taking place within the confessional are directly linked to the Sacred Heart of Jesus.

His Sacredness flows forth in an unstoppable tsunami of forgiveness and compassion.

This arterial lifeline of love flows from the Sacred Heart of Jesus into our now rejuvenated soul and quite often produces a feeling of relief, calm and happiness.

Again, this relief is a signal grace from God showing you that your sins truly are forgiven. It means that the previous scars in your soul are now erased. Therefore, if you died at that very moment you could very well be taken straight into heaven, especially if it happened on Divine Mercy Sunday.

Consequently, we must look at the heart again.

Our Confession must be truly heartfelt and with true repentance in our soul. God sees this anyway. You can't fool Him.

If there is no true repentance, the priest can sometimes refuse to give absolution.

So, as we can see, everything flows out from the Sacred Heart of Jesus.

The vibrancy of the Heart of Jesus produces Love.

"Love is everything," as Saint Paul says.

The Love of God is all powerful. It is His free gift to us. Accept this gift with both hands and spread it everywhere.

Chapter 10
Love

Love can be synonymous with the heart.

This comparison is not too obvious at first, but if we look deeper into this connection, we can be surprised about what comes to the surface.

For instance, when we look at modern day Valentine cards, we see a card emblazoned with hearts and the words "I love You."

So modern day romanticism seems inextricably linked to the bonding of love and hearts.

But where do we *feel* love?

Is it in our mind, or is it in our heart?

Again, the mind seems to be linked to the heart. I'm not a doctor or a psychologist, but it seems to me that there are definite linkups.

For instance, how many times have we heard the saying, "it was love at first sight."

So, sight reacts to something that is attractive and warming.

The mind that is linked to the heart reacts to the almost instantaneous visual receptivity of the eyes, receiving some sort of positive signal.

It brings us back to the arterial lifeline that I spoke about earlier in the book. This emotional signal is somehow embedded in the hearts of everyone. And seems to be transferred or pumped to the vital organs of our body.

This brings us once again to the very heart of the matter.

When a person receives a heart transplant, it is quite a common occurrence that the actual recipient of the transplanted heart, can actually sense a new type of feeling or physical trait that is different from what he or she can remember prior to the heart operation.

So, this implies that the new heart sometimes continues to pulsate with the previous owners physical and emotional characteristics, therefore suggesting how powerful the heart really is.

It should tell us that a heart can actually be embedded with 'feelings,' and memory signals.

I mentioned in my previous book, *You Are Mine Now*, that my Uncle Jimmy when he died was actually diagnosed with the condition of a 'broken heart.'

Apparently, the autopsy revealed a swollen heart which could only have been produced by a longing for something or someone in my uncle's life; which just happened to be my aunt Alice, who had died a couple of years before my uncle.

Now we are beginning to see a pattern of the complexities of our own hearts, both in the physical and emotional sense.

Somehow, this tells me that not only can a human heart be scarred, but this leads inextricably to the obvious link to a scarred soul which I also spoke about earlier.

A scarred soul, you may ask?

I once heard this true story about a close relative who had been deeply in love with a girl when he was in his early twenties.

He never did seem to get over the traumatic split-up.

Many years later he would receive dreams about his ex-girlfriend.

Through the years, due to God incidents, it was revealed to him that these dreams were actually true.

During the very last dream he received about his ex-girlfriend he heard a voice say, "I'm leaving now!"

He deduced in discernment that maybe his ex-girlfriend who had remarried was now spiritually leaving this earth. In other words, she was dying.

What all of this is suggesting to me; his heart and soul actually fused together almost like the enormous heat that is synonymous and akin to the powerful burning effect of a red-hot poker.

Once again this is building a pattern of the complexities of the human heart and soul.

Is Jesus complex?

Nope.

So, what does all of this tell us?

It should tell us that the infinite mind of God is sublime.

After all, he created us in love to glorify and obey his commandments.

If we can imagine looking at the road map of Britain.

Road lines everywhere.

If we can imagine looking at the rail links for Britain, rail links are everywhere.

If we can imagine looking at flight patterns of all the different airlines throughout Britain, flight paths are everywhere.

If we can imagine all these road, rail, and air links merging together throughout Britain, it can show us the complexities of modern-day travel.

In a sense, the road and rail links can be used as an analogy of the vast network of human veins and arteries in the human body.

The Channel tunnel can bring a further analogy.

The tunnel allows the trains and cars to spread out to Europe to the most outer extremities of European countries, almost like the arms and legs of our human body.

The Channel tunnel literally becomes the aorta (the main heart artery) of all existing destinations to Europe.

Without the aorta, the human heart and valves would not pulsate properly. Causing congestion and distress and literal death to the transport system.

We can only marvel at the wonderful design of the human body.

And yet look at how God has inbuilt HIS gift of emotions, feelings, intellect, and love throughout not only our bodies but throughout our human existence.

I never cease to marvel at how we can increase our fitness levels by constant exercise and dedication.

God allows us to think that we are actually helping ourselves by these human endeavours.

But actually, what is happening is this: God's gift is the human body, which at the moment of birth is a perfect miracle.

He asks us to try and keep His gifted body in good working order; why?

Because He needs us to be reasonably fit to help complete His work here on earth.

Of course, we have the victim souls, who experience great hardships here on earth to further the Kingdom of God. But that is God's choice and not ours. Who are we to question total love?

It's keeping perspective and balance in all our endeavours to help Jesus, His son.

Keep fit for God.

Keep active for Jesus.

This will ensure a constant and healthy arterial blood flow.

Chapter 11
Most Sacred Heart of Jesus,
I place all my trust in you

Do we really?

Dedication to the Sacred Heart of Jesus has been very popular in Catholic churches throughout the years.

This First Friday devotion emerged after Jesus appeared to Saint Margaret Mary Alacoque in 1673 (described earlier).

Jesus actually permitted Saint Margaret Mary to rest her head on His Sacred Heart during one of the apparitions (27th December 1673, on the feast of Saint John).

Just imagine that!

Being able to hear the Saviour's Heart pounding away.

I bet Saint Margaret Mary's ear was never quite the same again!

Listening, pondering about…Our Lord's sacred words.

His loving and tender words would have seared the heart of Saint Margaret Mary, almost welding her own privileged heart to the miraculous words of Jesus.

Here comes the crunch:

Do we, or can we really *trust* Jesus?

Let's look at the meaning of trust in the dictionary.

According to the KJV Dictionary, trust means; "Confidence, a reliance or resting of the mind on the integrity, veracity, justice and friendship or other sound principle of another person."

Already in this chapter, we can see something interesting emerging from the fact that Saint Margaret Mary Rested her head on the Sacred Heart of Jesus.

Let's dissect the meaning of *trust* in the dictionary. If we look closely at the first part of the dictionary commentary "....a reliance or RESTING OF THE MIND."

That's exactly what Saint Margaret Mary did. She rested her head on the Heart of Jesus. Her *mind* connected.

Secondly, she knew instinctively about the *Integrity* of Jesus.

Thirdly, the JUSTICE and FRIENDSHIP of Jesus were immediately apparent.

It's almost as if the dictionary explanation was written by Jesus Himself!

Can we rest our mind in the Sacred Heart of Jesus?

Can we be at ease with Him as a friend and comforter?

Can we truly rest our heart on His Sacred Heart?

Can we truly trust Him?

We really need to look at all these questions seriously.

How many times have we seen wonderful photographs of a mother and child together? It's breathtaking when we see the child rest his or her head on the bosom of the mother.

It immediately communicates closeness and tenderness.

No words are needed to explain the bond of two hearts lovingly brought together in a tender moment of both spiritual connection and supernatural grace.

The Heart of Jesus transcends the meaning of trust and sacredness. It emits unseen rays of love and hope to those who will truly open up to the graces that are freely available from the Saviour.

My very first school was located in Bridgeton, Glasgow.

And it just so happens that the name of my school was *The Sacred Heart*.

Before school registration, I attended Holy Mass most mornings in that Sacred Heart Chapel. The ornate altar and chapel surroundings remain a vivid part of my childhood memories.

It also brings back other areas of love and blessings that were bestowed upon me without me even realising it at that young age.

It surely was a blessing to enter that chapel and, in hindsight and gratitude, I thank Our Lord and His most Sacred Heart for instilling His presence in my heart from such an early age.

Our Lord's love for us is supernatural.

It prompts me to ask the question, What is love?

Some people have a love of possessions. Some love their countries. A bride can love her husband, and a groom, his bride. Sadly, there are those who love no one but themselves.

Therefore, can we define love?

God is the only one who can love perfectly.

So how does the Word of God define love?

If you are ever in any doubt about what love is, we only need to look at the book of Saint John:

"This is how God showed his love among us: He sent his one and only son into the world that we might live through him. This is Love: not that we loved God, but that he loved us and sent his son as an atoning sacrifice for our sins." (John: 9-10 NIV)

Jesus's cross is the perfect expression of God's love.

Although an instrument of torture and brutal violence, the cross has become the greatest and most potent sign of God's love.

When Jesus hung and bled and suffered, it was God saying to every human being "I love you."

Saint Paul only boasted of one thing: "the Cross."

In the cross, he discovered the depth, length and width of God's love.

"As for me, the only thing I can boast about is the cross of our Lord Jesus Christ." (Gal. 6:4)

Taking God's love a bit further, Saint John says:

"My dear people, let us Love one another since Love comes from God, and everyone who loves is begotten by God and knows God. Anyone who fails to love can never have known God. Because, God is love..."

The sacredness of God's all-consuming love is directly linked to His Son's most Sacred Heart which beats every minute of every day for the sins of all mankind.

Chapter 12
Consecration to the
Sacred Heart of Jesus

Sacred Heart of Jesus, filled with infinite love broken by my ingratitude, pierced by my sins, yet loving me still.

Accept the consecration that I make to You of all that I am and all that I have.

Take every faculty of my soul and body and draw me day by day nearer and nearer to Your Sacred side.

And there as I can bear the lesson, teach me Your blessed ways.

Chapter 13
The Sacred Heart

In art, the Sacred Heart is pierced, surmounted by a cross, and encircled with thorns. Light radiates from it to show that it is a burning furnace of love. The heart of Christ summarises the paschal mystery – the death and resurrection of Jesus – that were prompted by divine love.

Your heart pumps about 100,000 times a day to keep your lifeblood flowing through you. For this reason, it has become a symbol for our very selves. The heart, as previously mentioned, has become a symbol for love, perhaps because it seems to beat faster when we are in love.

The biblical image of the heart means the depth of ourselves, where we decide for or against God.

God, who always speaks to us using our own experiences, has chosen our symbol of the heart to represent Jesus.

Jesus said that from within Him would flow streams of living water (John 7:38), referring to the Holy Spirit. The water from the side of Christ on the cross was the water of salvation, the Holy Spirit. This sacred living water saturates us, forming a powerful devotion to the Sacred Heart that focuses not only on the love and mercy Jesus has for us but on reparation for sin.

In Saint Margaret Mary's visions, Christ requested that a Communion of reparation be made on the first Friday of every month. An organisation called the Apostleship of Prayer furthers the devotion to the Sacred Heart through activities such as the enthronement of the Sacred Heart in homes. We pray that our hearts may become like the Heart of Christ.

In 1675 on the feast of Corpus Christi (the Body and Blood of Christ), Christ showed Saint Margaret Mary His wounded heart. He said, "Behold this heart burning with so great a love for men."

In 1856 a feast in honour of the Sacred Heart was set for the Friday after the feast of the Body and Blood of Christ. In 1899 Pope Leo XIII dedicated the world to the Sacred Heart.

The heart of Jesus was a human heart like ours. It stopped beating the day Jesus was crucified. According to the Gospel of John, after Jesus had died, a soldier made sure of his death by piercing His side with a lance. Blood and water ran out (19:34). Jesus's pierced heart became a sign of the completeness of His love for us, a love that compelled Him to die for us and that prompted Him to remain with us in the bread and wine of the Eucharist. The physical heart of Jesus is the symbol of the total love of Jesus, divine and human.

Chapter 14
Miserentissimus Redemptor

The Holy See has given this devotion a high place of importance in the Church due not only to the requests of Jesus to Saint Margaret Mary but also to the soundness of the doctrine and its timeliness in rekindling love and trust in the Merciful Heart of Our Saviour. Pope Pius XI, in the encyclical *Miserentissimus Redemptor*, writes about the meaning of the vision of The Sacred Heart.

"He showed his heart to us bearing about it the symbols of the passion and displaying the flames of love, that from the one we might know the infinite malice of sin, and in the other we might admire the infinite charity of Our Redeemer, and so might have a more vehement hatred of sin, and make a more ardent return of love for His Love."

In this encyclical, Pope Pius stressed that reparation to The Sacred Heart is obligatory for all Christians. He ends his encyclical stating that "the devotion of reparation to the Sacred Heart has the highest approval of Apostolic Authority and must be practised universally by all."

Following the writings and visions of Saint Margaret Mary and Saint Claude La Colombière, many popes have written on the immense importance of devotion to The Sacred Heart, including : Leo XIII, Benedict XV, Pius XII, John XXIII, Paul V1, John Paul II.

On the 50th anniversary of Pope Pius XII's encyclical *Haurietis Aquas* on devotion to the Sacred Heart, Pope Benedict wrote, This devotion (to the Sacred Heart) is "the contemplation of the 'side pierced with the spear,' in which shines the limitless will of salvation on the part of God."

For this reason, it cannot be considered as a passing form of worship or devotion. Adoration of the love of God, which was found in the symbol of the 'pierced heart' is a historical – devotional expression, continuing to be vital for a living relationship with God."

Chapter 15
A Broader Meaning

The devotion to the Divine Mercy given to Saint Faustina Kowalska in 1931 is really a broadened devotion to the Sacred Heart.

From this devotion our trust in God's limitless love and mercy is rekindled. The incomprehensible treasures that we have in the sacraments are symbolised in the blood and water gushing forth from the Heart of Christ. The devotion to the Sacred Heart has flowered and has seemed to come full circle in the devotion to the Divine Mercy, particularly in its emphasis on the graces flowing from the Heart of Jesus, healing and forgiving souls, through the Sacraments of Mercy.

Devotion to the Sacred Heart can be seen as early as the second century with Saint Justyn Martyr and in the 7th century with Pope Gregory the Great. Writers throughout these centuries emphasized the pierced side of Christ as the inexhaustible source from which all graces flow upon mankind and the blood and water as symbols of the Sacraments of the Church.

With the coming of Saint Bernard of Clairvaux and Saint Anselm in the 12th century, there was a sudden increase in direct reference to the love of The Sacred Heart for every person redeemed by His Passion and Death. The widespread influence of Franciscan and Dominican Friars enkindled this devotion in the hearts of the faithful who heard their preaching. The focus on the Sacred Heart moved from being a symbol of the Sacraments, to the symbol of Divine Love.

One cannot pass over the Middle Ages without mentioning Saints Gertrude and Mechtilde. The editor of Saint Gertrude's writings, Revelations (Dom Boutras of Solesmes) stated: "Never before...has anything been written on the effect of the Divine Heart and its relation to men, to saints, to the Souls in Purgatory, such as we find in the writings of Saint Gertrude and Saint Mechtilde."

The contemplation of the Humanity of Christ in his Passion, devotion to the Blessed Eucharist (in particular, the feast of Corpus Christi) and the surge in mysticism gave the devotion to the Sacred Heart a new vitality in the middle ages. Prior to the revelations to Saint Margaret Mary religious communities, particularly in France, continued to spread devotion to the Sacred Heart of Jesus throughout the world.

The French spiritual leaders paved the way for the message given to Saint Margaret Mary Alacoque.

Saint Margaret Mary entered the Daughters of The Visitation, founded by Saint Francis de Sales and Saint Jane Frances de Chantal in 1671.

Although devotion to the Heart of Jesus was already important to the order prior to Saint Margaret Mary's entrance, it would be through her that public devotion to the Sacred Heart (reparation, consecration and a liturgical feast) would be practised universally in the Catholic Church. Saint Francis de Sales wrote, "Our little congregation is the work of the Hearts of Jesus and Mary. Our dying Saviour gave birth to us by the wound in his Sacred Heart." Saint Jane told her daughters, "Pray that your heart may be made like to the heart of Jesus."

It was to this order that Jesus gave the deepest knowledge of His Sacred Heart and the express command to spread devotion to it.

During this time, the heresy of Jansenism was spreading like wildfire throughout Europe. The Jansenists instilled fear into the hearts of the faithful, turning the religion of faith and love into one of pessimism and scrupulosity, teaching that man is completely incapable of disposing himself to the grace offered by God. Frequent Communion was also frowned upon.

In contrast to the Jansenists, between the years of 1673 and 1675 Jesus appeared to Saint Margaret Mary revealing his Divine Heart to her. In one apparition he told her, "My Divine Heart is so passionately in love with humanity and with you, in particular, that it cannot keep back the pent-up flames of its burning charity any longer. They must burst out through you."

Our Lord mourned the indifference and ingratitude of the greater part of humanity.

It's interesting to note Our Lord's words: "that it cannot keep back the pent-up flames of its burning charity any longer."

During the second world war, the flame thrower was a powerful weapon during warfare seeking by the flames from this incinerating war machine to burn up the poor recipients of this deadly war tool. This somewhat horror-filled analogy shows us the power and directness of the Saviour's loving words. Through the example of these powerful statements from Jesus, it directly shows us, the pent-up flames and the burning charity he felt for us.

Saint Margaret Mary was a cloistered nun and so to help her carry out the mission entrusted to her, Our Lord brought Saint Claude La Colombière (a Jesuit priest) to her to be her Spiritual Director. He was the first to believe in the revelations of the Sacred Heart to Saint Margaret Mary.

Thanks to his support, her superior also believed, and widespread propagation of the devotion to the Sacred Heart began in the universal church. From then on, the Jesuits became the chief propagators of the devotion to the Sacred Heart which flourished throughout the subsequent centuries.

Reference: https://sacredheartbasilica.com/history-and-devotion-of-the-sacred-heart-of-jesus

Chapter 16
Heart Unto Heart

Sound familiar?

Saint John Paul II, speaking two millennia after the death of Jesus, said, "The worst prison is a closed heart." Those who resisted Jesus refused to open up their minds and ultimately their hearts to the work of God in their midst.

As Antoine de Saint Exupery once said, "It is only with the heart that one can see rightly; what is essential is invisible to the human eye."

Moving further on, we look at Cardinal John Henry Newman.

He was a parish priest who was deeply loved by all who knew him. He was a man who understood that mind and heart had to go together in the great enterprises of life, the greatest of which is the search for God and for that life-giving relationship with him. Newman spoke and wrote eloquently of this inner personal search and of the joy it brings. He expressed the emptiness of life without God in these terms: "If I looked into a mirror, and did not see my face, I should have the sort of feeling which actually comes upon me, when I look into this busy world, and see no reflection of its Creator."

Pope Benedict XVI, on his visit to the UK on the 16th September 2010, chose the same motto as Cardinal

Newman's coat of arms, "Heart Speaks Unto Heart."

How often have we felt that a good heart-to-heart discussion has solved the problems of intransigence and bitterness?

And yet, religious bitterness can be generational, being handed down from generation to generation.

We only have to look at the local Old Firm Match of Celtic and Rangers here in Scotland to realise that the enormous problem of religious bigotry is still alive and well.

(A few years ago, I worked with the anti-sectarian group called 'Nil By Mouth').

Unfortunately, in our society the phonetic sounds that come from our mouths can wreck lives in both a social and personal context.

We can only come to the fount of love and mercy by imploring God's mercy, even though we can be cold and so ungrateful.

Unfold to us the treasures of thy grace, that so our hearts may long to gaze upon thy face in eternity.

Let us follow the print of thy dear footsteps, and when we fall, Sweet Heart of Jesus, continue to love us still.

Chapter 17
Connections to The Divine Mercy

Contained within Saint Faustina's Diary called, *Divine Mercy In My Soul,* there are many references and connections to Our Lord's Sacred Heart;

Here are just a few, Notebook I No 186

I desire that you know more profoundly the love that burns in my Heart for souls, and you will understand this when you meditate on My Passion. Call upon my Mercy on behalf of sinners; I desire their salvation. When you say this prayer with a contrite heart and with faith on behalf of some sinner, I will give him the grace of conversion this is the prayer:

"O Blood and Water which gushed forth from the HEART of Jesus I Trust in you."

Notebook I No 282

My Heart was moved by great mercy towards you. My dearest child when I saw you turn to shreds because of the great pain you suffered in repenting for your sins. I saw your love, so pure and true that I give you first place among the virgins. You are the honour and glory of My Passion. I see every abasement of your soul, and nothing escapes my attention. I lift up the humble even to My very throne, because I want it so.

Notebook II No 866

My daughter I want to repose in your Heart, because many souls have thrown me out of their hearts today. I have experienced sorrow unto death.

Notebook III No 1074

The flames of mercy are burning me. I desire to pour them out upon human souls. Oh, what pain they cause Me when they do not want to accept them!

My daughter, do whatever is within your power to spread devotion to My mercy. I will make up for what you lack. Tell aching mankind to snuggle close to my merciful Heart, and I will fill it with peace.

Notebook III No 1228 (Ninth Day of Divine Mercy Novena)

Today bring to Me souls who have become lukewarm, and immerse them in the abyss of My mercy. These souls wound my Heart most painfully. My soul suffered the most dreadful loathing in the Garden of Olives because of lukewarm souls. They were the reason I cried out: "Father, take this cup away from me, if it be your will." For them, the last hope of salvation is to flee to My mercy.

Notebook V No 1485

My mercy is greater than your sins and those of the entire world. Who can measure the extent of my goodness? For you I descended from heaven to earth; for you I allowed myself to be nailed to the cross; for you I let my Sacred Heart be pierced with a lance, thus opening wide the source of mercy for you.

Come then, with trust to draw graces from this fountain. I never reject a contrite heart. Your misery has disappeared in the depths of My mercy. Do not argue with Me about your wretchedness. You will give me pleasure if you hand over to me all your troubles and griefs. I shall heap upon you the treasures of My grace.

Notebook V No 1521

My daughter, do not tire of proclaiming My mercy. In this way you will refresh this Heart of Mine, which burns with a flame of pity for sinners. Tell My priests that hardened sinners will repent on hearing their words when they speak about My unfathomable mercy, about the compassion I have for them in My Heart. To priests who proclaim and extol My mercy, I will give wondrous power; I will anoint their words and touch the hearts of those to whom they will speak.

These excerpts from *Saint Faustina's Diary* show a strong link to the Sacred Heart of Jesus and prove that his mercy is truly unfathomable.

Chapter 18
Entwined Love

Love is entwined in the heart ….it cannot be separated. Forever joined by the power of Abba Father, for He is the Creator of Love and is Love itself.

Never be perplexed by this, it goes to say that all our actions from the very source of life are guided by enormous pulsating signal graces that flow every moment of the day.

All we have to do is tap into this wonderful free gift from God, a gift that really is as startling and revelatory as the Bible itself.

Every moment of our lives is watched tenderly by God the Father. He doesn't overlook anybody. We just need to connect. It's like an electrical unit in our homes. Take for instance a common everyday Hoover vacuum. It won't operate or clean a dirty carpet until it is plugged in to the freely available electrical source.

If we look at the love that is freely available from Abba, it makes sense to 'plug in' or nothing works!

So how do we plug in? That's the question.

We must imagine our very own human heart attached to the Sacred Heart of Jesus. That each beat we hear from our own heart is being pumped by a supernatural force –

unseen, yet powerful.

This realisation will set off a chain reaction of wonderment and appreciation, knowing that even our very words can be guided by Jesus, if we truly act in love.

We can hurt the Sacred Heart of Jesus when we act unjustly and treat others with disdain and ridicule.

To heighten our awareness of Jesus living within us, it only takes a couple of seconds to ask ourselves this important question – what would Jesus do in this situation?

Throughout the Gospels, Jesus stayed silent when rebuked.

But he also worked as the Master of justice. Justice comes from the Sacred Heart. It is sovereign. Jesus could bring those who were determined to kill Him to their knees with a sharp retort or a most loving glance.

Many times, He was told not to heal on the sabbath, but He told them that He was in command of the sabbath.

Imagine telling the Saviour NOT to heal.

How weak mankind can be.

We are all flawed creatures. Abba Father knew what He was doing when He gave each person an individual will. But more importantly, this will is a FREE gift.

If we didn't have free will, we would be robots – it's as simple as that. Yet the scoffers and the atheists say, "Why does God allow worldwide disasters and famines?"

The answer is simple. Man is at the root of famines, war and the like. We only have to look at the forced famine in Russia in the early 1900's that killed over ten million people.

God wants all of His children to be safe. He wants all of us to come home safely to Him in heaven.

Just like our beating hearts, in order to function properly, the pumped blood must return to the heart and then continue to flow through our arteries in an unceasing and pulsating circuit of love.

This circuit of love links directly towards the overflowing tenderness of God's beating omnipotence that shines out throughout the galaxies and universes and ultimately covers the whole of the earth with a radiance that shines brighter than the sun.

However, radiance can be blocked out in a number of different ways.

Some people turn away from love. Some people shun affection. Others will actually cause harm through a vicious tongue which normally ends in violence.

That is when the Hoover breaks down. There is a malfunction which stops the flow of electricity to the heart of the machine.

Then we need repairs.

This is where the Sacrament of Reconciliation comes in.

Our hearts and minds can be adjusted through true

repentance to Our Saviour. Only then can the internal workings of our souls be restored to health.

Oh, for a good electrician!

We already have the Greatest Electrician the world has ever seen. He can repair hundreds and thousands of human Hoovers at the same time!

So, let us keep the human Hoover working at all times by frequent Confession. That way, any form of malfunction or breakdown is minimised.

The oil that a Hoover needs to function can be likened to the mini-exorcism contained within the absolution at the end of Confession.

That exorcism prayer keeps us moving along the path of our human existence, just like the working parts of the Hoover.

Another analogy: the main function of the Hoover is to suck up dirt. Confession takes away the dirt of our sins.

As said earlier, we are all sinners. But if we don't Hoover up those sins in Confession, then all we end up with are dirty carpets.

Chapter 19
The Heart in the Biblical Sense

"Finding himself in the midst of a battlefield man has to struggle to do what is right, and it is at great cost to himself, and aided by God's grace, that he succeeds in achieving his own inner integrity." (*Gaudium et Spes* 37)

Hoovering up our sins, (as stated in the previous chapter), also needs God's grace.

The German theologian Dietrich Bonhoeffer, who was executed by the Nazis days before the end of the second world war, said "The heart in the biblical sense is not the inward life, but the whole person in relation to God."

This insight helps us to understand that when the Bible speaks of the heart, it is referring to something very profound about our identity as persons. Whereas it is impossible for us to know what is in each other's hearts, or even, if we are honest, in our own, the Bible tells us
"for the Lord sees not as man sees, man looks on the outward appearance, but the Lord looks on the heart." (1 Sam. 16:7)

Since the Lord looks at our hearts, we need to ask ourselves the question, what is in our hearts?

Jesus answers this question very clearly. If we look at the reading from Mark 7:14-23, the explanation explodes in our face. "For from within, out of the heart of man, come evil thoughts, fornication, theft, murder, adultery, coveting, wickedness, deceit, licentiousness, envy, slander, pride and foolishness." (21-22)

There is a dark side to the human heart which can be hard to accept.

Jesus is an expert on humanity. He knows us, He created us.

We are a fallen creation in need of redemption.

Our lives are a conflict between good and evil, and the battleground lies in our hearts.

The acceptance of our fallen condition does not come naturally but is itself an acceptance of grace.

The truth is, that each one of us is a fallen human being who leans too easily and readily towards what is wrong and dark, and without God's grace, would fall into all types of rebellion and sin.

While we may struggle to acknowledge this truth, we need to come to the point where we are able to confess the state of our hearts before God.

Only God can purify our Hearts; only the Holy Spirit can liberate us from the darkness within; and only by prayer, reading God's word and receiving the sacraments do we embark on the road to holiness and purity of heart.

The greatest obstacle to receiving God's grace is pride. The very minute we feel that a fall can never happen, it happens.

We must be on our guard, putting on the armour of God at all times.

If we confess that we are truly weak sinners, this is probably the biggest grace that we will ever receive from Jesus.

Then God can truly work through the weakness in our Heart.

The almighty compassion of Jesus is beyond all understanding but let's grasp this amazing grace with both hands and place our own heart within the Sacred Heart of Jesus.

That way we can safely rest our own troubled hearts within the almighty beating heart of Jesus, and rest in the knowledge that Jesus is in control of our destiny.

Many saints rested within the Sacred Heart of Jesus too.

Chapter 20
Saints Aligned to
The Sacred Heart

Here are just a few saints whose lives were deeply connected to the Sacred Heart of Jesus.

Saint Gertrude (1256-1302)

Saint Gertrude encouraged others to pray to the Sacred Heart of Jesus for graces. Jesus told her, "They may draw forth all they need from my Divine Heart." (Re: National Catholic Register)

Saint Maximilian Kolbe (1894-1941)

Total consecration to the Immaculate. Saint Maximilian knew that as soon as the Immaculate was known to all hearts, the Kingdom of the Sacred Heart would reign in the world. (Wikipedia)

Saint Frances Cabrini (1850-1917)

Mother Cabrini was an Italian American religious sister who founded the Missionary Sisters of the Sacred Heart. (Wikipedia)

Saint Mechtilde of Hackeborn (1241-1298)

Saint Mechtilde became an ardent promoter of devotion to the Sacred Heart of Jesus. She was a Benedictine Nun. (Mechtilde – Wikipedia)

Saint Lutgardis of Aywieres (1182-1246)

Saint Lutgardis was one of the great precursors of the devotion to the Sacred Heart of Jesus.

The first recorded mystical revelation of Christ's Heart is that of Saint Lutgardis. (wiki-visually)

Saint Louis-Marie De Montfort (1673-1716)

Saint Louis de Montfort promoted and spread devotion to the Sacred Heart of Jesus – to a far greater extent, than is generally realised. (Sacred Heart Alliance)

Aspiration to The Sacred Heart of Jesus

O Sacred Heart of Jesus, I place all my trust in thee.

Jesus, meek and humble of heart, make my heart like unto thine.

May the Sacred Heart of Jesus be loved for evermore.

Love of the Heart of Jesus, inflame my heart.

Charity of the Heart of Jesus, flow into my heart.

Strength of the Heart of Jesus, support my heart.

Mercy of the Heart of Jesus, pardon my heart.

Patience of the Heart of Jesus, do not weary of my heart.

Wisdom of the Heart of Jesus, teach my heart.

Cœur de Jésus Sts-Gervais-Protais

Chapter 21
Change of Heart

Unfortunately, there is always a flip side to every sentiment regarding the heart.

If we look at Jeremiah 17 starting at Verse 5, we see the flip side very clearly.

"The Lord says this:

'A curse on the man who puts his trust in man, who relies on things of the flesh whose Heart turns from the Lord. He is like dry scrub in the wastelands: if good comes he has no eyes for it, he settles in the parched places of the wilderness, a salt land, uninhabited. A blessing on the man who puts his trust in the Lord, with the Lord for his hope. He is like a tree by the waterside that thrusts its roots to the stream : when the heat comes it feels no alarm, its foliage stays green; it has no worries in a year of drought, and never ceases to bear fruit. The heart is more devious than any other thing, perverse too: who can pierce its secrets?

I, the Lord, search to the heart, I probe the loins, to give each man what his conduct and his actions deserve. The partridge will hatch eggs it has not laid. Similarly, the man who wins his wealth unjustly: his days half done, he must leave it, proving a fool after all.'"

Let's look at the sentence, "the heart is more devious than any other thing."

The heart, especially on Saint Valentine's Day cards, is viewed with tenderness and love. And yet here we have

Jeremiah tearing that notion apart, showing us that the heart can be truly devious.

In previous chapters, I have spoken about the very uniqueness of the human heart, how it works and how it provides a lifeline to other parts of the human body.

But here we see the emotional depth that a devious heart will sink to. There is nothing that gets in the way of someone who is hell-bent on causing hurt mayhem and absolute evil in another person's life.

We see these patterns in everyday life. Just pick up a newspaper, and we notice the havoc that is caused: murders, rape, all kinds of horrible actions. Most of these originate from a devious heart and mind.

If people would stop to think, who created the heart, this marvel of perfection?

Jesus in His humanity tells us that He is in our Hearts.

But even Jesus, because of our freedom of will, cannot overtake a heart that is hell-bent on destruction. Sure, he can bring about good from evil; this has been proven many times. But at that very moment of evil intent, the evil one seems to take over. Just look at the example of Judas, when the scriptures tell us, "Satan entered him." (John 13: 27)

Therefore, a good heart seems to need the guidance of a good disciplined prayer life and strict adherence to the sacraments.

This is not to say that people who are away from their faith cannot have a good heart. I know people who purport to be atheists, and yet still have a friendly and kind nature. But, do they recognise where the kindness is coming from? That's the question.

The recognition of the very existence of Jesus in our hearts is definitely enhanced by our spiritual journey and strong adherence to the holy words of the Bible.

The Book of Jeremiah unearths the very question of a devious heart. It lets us see the human weakness in every person on God's good earth.

Chapter 22
Let's Get to the
Heart of the Matter

Today's date is March 23rd, 2020, and because of the existing coronavirus pandemic, Prime Minister Boris Johnston has just announced a three-week lockdown on the whole of the UK.

Terms such as "self-isolation" and "social distancing" are now part of the very fabric of our daily lives.

Who would have thought that barely a year ago there was nothing on the horizon that could have predicted the emergence of this worldwide virus?

Almost daily we are hearing about the fatalities, particularly among the elderly. It seems that people with pre-existing conditions such as serious heart and lung conditions are most at risk.

At present there's a total of 14,366 deaths because of the coronavirus, and this statistic is constantly rising.

What are we to make of this catastrophic world-wide health crisis?

Is God showing us something?

Maybe the Sacred Heart of our Creator is losing patience with the human race.

Meanwhile, the world – it seems – is pushing the self-destruct button.

Saint Mother Teresa once said, "until the carnage and outright murder of innocent babies in the womb, through the evil of abortion stops – there will be no peace."

Think about it. God's creations of love are being destroyed by the selfish and inhumane actions of the 'my body' proponents of outright genocide.

It is ironic that the "in" terms of "self-isolating" and "social distancing" are distinctly linked to the "lost" babies.

Through abortion, there is distinct "social distancing" from the innocent babies in the womb.

The "self-isolating" of the babies in the womb by the abortionists is a direct result of the vicious spiral of demonic intuition, induced by the evil one.

Yes, Satan is powerful, cunning, and relentless.

But, I have news for him. His reign is coming to an end.

There is a story coming out of Italy about atheistic doctors who are being converted to Jesus.

Italy is almost on its knees because of the coronavirus, but some doctors in a hospital were amazed when an infected elderly pastor was seen reading the Bible to his fellow patients.

Through sheer exhaustion, the atheistic doctors started to listen to the man. As the pastor was reading the Bible to his fellow patients, the doctors began to notice and feel a distinct peace emanating around the ward. Some of the doctors, through the actions of this elderly pastor, became believers!

Unfortunately, the elderly man died of the virus, but his work was done, and through the miracle of these conversions, Jesus took him home to his heavenly reward.

So even in the midst of this viral darkness, the magnificent light of Christ the King will shine through. (Re: from an Italian doctor in Italy March 2020, "From Atheist to Humble Believer.")

Another button of destruction being pressed is the absolute selfishness which is very prevalent during these trying times. Does the general public see how deadly the virus of self-seeking really is?

As an example, just look at the newspaper pictures of empty supermarket shelves: absolute panic-buying of precious commodities and food stuffs. Not thinking of anyone but their own selfish motives.

Added to all of this is the chaos being caused by the present gender politically correct (PC) brigade.

God Made Man.

God Made Woman. Full Stop, End of Story.

Maybe the isolation in homes will make people think about their lives and their futures.

Maybe non-believers will say a prayer like the doctors in

Italy.

Maybe the secularists will begin to realise that God is in control, not them.

We are even reading that couples in long-term partnerships in the UK are being advised to stay in separate houses to stop the spread of the coronavirus.

Is God telling the "live-in" couples to look at their relationships and get married?

Lord Jesus, saturate us with Your Healing Precious Blood now and forever.

Chapter 23
Solitude and Self Isolation

As we stumble through these uncertain times, all of humanity is being asked direct and disturbing questions. Am I comfortable in my own skin? Will I really get to know my own self?

To self-isolate – as we are being told by the government – is to strictly adhere to the guidelines. Social exclusion, everything points to a new way of looking at life.

We are allowed out of our homes for light exercise and visiting shops. We can't visit our grandchildren.

Stay away from human contact unless it is vitally important. All these new rules will certainly challenge our normal way of life. But emotionally, will it affect us?

I spoke to a priest friend yesterday, and he told me how the self-isolation is affecting him. "I seem to be experiencing more peace." Continuing, he said, "I am now going on a self-imposed retreat."

So here we have an isolated priest, reversing the trend to panic and worry, and utilising this God-given time of solitude and putting it to good use.

Look at Jesus in the Garden of Gethsemane, the isolation, the almost unbearable solitude. He asked the Father to "take away this cup." His human fear came to the surface.

Just as we see fear today. The uncertainty of the future.

Are we being tested? Is the present crisis some form of chastisement? So many questions, without an answer.

All I can say is this this: Anne Graham Lotz, the daughter of Billy Graham, the famous evangelist, was asked a question by Jane Clayson of the CBS Early Show, on September 13th 2001, not long after the 9/11 terrorist attack on the twin towers in New York: "How could God let this happen?" Jane asked.

Anne Graham Lotz replied, "I believe God is deeply saddened by this, just as we are. But, for years we've been telling God to get out of our schools, to get out of our government and to get out of our lives. And, being the gentleman that he is, I believe he has calmly backed out."

What a profound answer.

I believe that these times we are living in are serious.

I honestly think we could class this era as being the 'end times.'

Whatever dates that God has in mind for the final battle against Satan, only He knows. But all around us, we can sense a supernatural shift in world events. Weather patterns, plagues, financial turmoil, and terrorism all point towards the future Armageddon.

Are we to blame?

As Anne Graham Lotz reminds us, we are certainly not

helping. But aligned to these facts is the flip side of the coin: where is Satan in all of this?

The coronavirus (at the moment) is gradually stripping away our spiritual heritage.

We can't go to Holy Mass.
We can't even go to Confession (unless it is privately organised).
No holy water in chapels.
The list goes on and on.

Who is gaining from all this dark chaos?

One simple answer, Satan.

Therefore, we must ask the question: Is the evil one prompting the almost unbelievable series of events that are taking place at this moment within the Holy Catholic Church?

There is only one conclusion, of course, he is.

Satan is absolutely delighted at the diabolical manifestations erupting all around us.

How can we stop what is happening?

By the power of the holy Rosary and fasting. In fact, Pope Francis will be giving a General Absolution to the whole world this Friday, the 27th March 2020 at six p.m. (Rome Time).

Jesus Christ is the Head of the Church.

Satan will never destroy the Church with Jesus as our leader. But we must *never* relax or become complacent. We can fight the negative fire of evil with the incredible fire of the Holy Spirit, and with a grace-filled determination to step up our prayer lives and really go on the offensive as true warriors of Christ The King.

Chapter 24
Hearts of Men

Our Divine Lord said to Saint Margaret Mary Alacoque in 1675, "Behold the heart which has so loved men, that it spared nothing...while in acknowledgement I get back nothing for the most part; but the ingratitude, contempt, irreverence, sacrileges, and coldness, which they show Me in the Sacrament of Love."

It is also true today.

The hearts of men have turned away from God.

They forget His love; they have no time for Him.

They forget that they should depend on Jesus for everything.

Even today when the churches fill up for Holy Mass, at the very solemn moment of consecration for the sins of mankind, men's hearts are still cold and unresponsive.

It is a special moment in time when we should thank Jesus for His wonderful love and compassion. We should really linger and deeply appreciate what is actually happening. We should kneel in reparation, and also offer Jesus our heart in devoted love, by saying; *"Jesus, I offer my life, family and all that I am to you. Take me in to your most compassionate Heart, and please let me reside with You forever."*

I can hear Jesus say, "Tell me your troubles."

Do we?

If we submit to Our Lord acknowledging that we are weak sinners, will He turn away from us?

Of course not. That's exactly what Jesus wants us to do: admit to our weakness, admit to our sins, and literally crawl to His majestic presence in all humility.

Then, the King of Kings steps in. He lavishes a supernatural forgiveness upon us. He drenches us in His most precious blood. He says to us, "Come to Me all you who are weary, and I will give you strength." (Math 11-28)

What immense love; can we replicate that form of love within ourselves? No, I don't think so. Only through the magnificent grace of Jesus can we attain the love that He wants us to share with each other.

His grace is sufficient for us; if we learn to recognise it and put it in to practice.

Let us learn to honour the wonderful Sacrament of His Divine love (Holy Communion).

Jesus's Divine Love is linked to His Sacred and Divine Heart…everything that emanates from Our Lord's Sacred Heart is truly supernatural, therefore when we receive Holy Communion, it is truly a special part of the Saviour's unconditional Heart that we are receiving. "Oh, sweet Jesus, Oh, Holy Jesus, may my heart be a lamp the light of which shall burn for You alone."

There is a special promise of salvation that was revealed to Saint Margaret Mary Alacoque. She says; "He then assured me that the pleasure He takes in being loved, known, and honoured by His creatures is so great, that He promised me that no one who has specially dedicated and consecrated himself to Him will ever perish."

There is only one word to describe that loving promise...wow.

Within the content of the previous page, I speak about the magnificent grace of Jesus. Our lives are a continuous conveyor belt of unseen graces; being freely and unconditionally given to us by the unfathomable Divine Mercy of Jesus.

Yes, that's right, Our Lord's Divine Mercy.

He actually allows us to think that sometimes we achieve our spiritual goals by ourselves!

And yet, the opposite is the case.

Jesus is essential in all our lives.

If we truly live a disciplined spiritual life, then the grace and guidance of Jesus is automatic in our lives.

I've seen it so many times in my own spiritual journey.

But what if we are not living a good spiritual life. Will Jesus still help us?

Of course, He does, He still helps us, albeit to a lesser extent. But the problem of a weak faith comes to the surface in a lack of judgement and a lack of discernment.

Many times those who are lacking in faith are shown divine examples of Jesus's unconditional love, but these people seem to overlook the divine grace given to them, and through their lack of discernment, the God-given graces go sailing by.

One example of God's grace given to someone who was lacking in real faith; but who still reached out to God at the last moment of his life. And that person was the thief on the cross at Our Lord's Crucifixion. (Luke 23:43)

He asked Jesus, when he saw the other criminal mocking Jesus; "Jesus, will you remember me when you come into your kingdom?"

And, of course, we should all know what Jesus's reply was; "Today you will be with me in paradise."

It shows us the unfathomable Divine Mercy of Jesus.

For me this is one of the most powerful scenes in the Gospels. Jesus is teaching us a big lesson in this powerful situation. No matter what your sins, as I said earlier, if you truly turn to Jesus and beg His help, He will help you.

And now a special prayer of Saint Ignatius, entitled *The Sume et Suscipe:*

"Take, O Lord, and receive my whole liberty, my memory, my understanding, and my will. Whatever I have and possess Thou hast given me. To Thee, O Lord, I restore them. They are all thine, dispose of them according to Thy Will. Give me only Thy love and Thy GRACE, and that is enough for me." (from *Hours with Jesus*, by Rev. P. Omara SJ)

What a wonderful prayer of surrender.

I've included it because the ultimate act of surrender – other than Our Lord's Sacrifice on the cross – was the total act of surrender by the thief.

So, surrender also seems to be a key element in spiritually bonding with the Sacred Heart of Jesus.

We cannot expect to merge with the loving heart of Jesus if we don't have the special grace of true surrender.

True surrender leads to an open heart.

An open heart leads to purity of prayer.

I will explain this in more detail in the next chapter.

Chapter 25
Praying With Your Heart

Jesus's Sacred Heart burns with love for all mankind.

He asks us to return that unconditional love with a love that duly repays His meekness, ardour, and sensitivity.

The goodness of a person's heart is manifested in their words and actions, which are the translation of good thoughts and of good works. These attributes are the tangible consequence of perfect surrender.

Surrender helps to prepare the heart for a purity of prayer and intention.

The good person fosters thoughts of peace towards everyone. They do not sow the seeds of disputes.

A good heart is compassionate towards all miseries, suffering with all who suffer, and weeping with the one who weeps, whilst not envying anyone; only wishing the good of others.

We should pray and ask for all these attributes. But these great qualities are already present in the most Sacred Heart of Jesus.

Therefore, it makes sense to believe that Jesus is just bursting to give us His love. To pour out His help and forgiveness. All we need to do is ask with a contrite heart, and it will be given to us unconditionally.

Jesus's Divine Heart is the heart of God since in Him resides the Divine Person of the Son of God.

We will never be able to understand the wonderful dimensions and virtues of His Divine Heart.

If we truly knew how great the love of God is for us, our lives would be entirely different. We would hate sin which offends Him, and we would combat evil under whatever form it presents to us.

We should rejoice in everything.

Jesus rejoiced in doing what His Father asked.

Our only worry should be to seek out the desires of the Heart of the Father, even to the smallest detail.

We should know that, in Jesus's Divine Heart, we can and should take up residence, enjoying the infinite tenderness of His love.

Even a tender mother cannot do everything on behalf of her children, but Jesus can.

Jesus wants all of us to come to His Heart, which is immense in its goodness, infinite in its grandeur and completely open to our pleading.

Children are particularly pleasing to Our Blessed Lord, and He desires to protect them from evil.

There is sadness in the Heart of Jesus when each child of age commits their first mortal sin.

Jesus is also calling the youth to His Sacred Heart. He wants them to consecrate themselves to His tenderness. This way, if they continue to surrender to His call, the supernatural drawing power of Jesus becomes irresistible.

The Heart of Jesus is always young, for God never grows old.

Albeit, a lot of youth scorn Jesus; they do not seem to understand Him, and that, in itself, keeps them separated from the Saviour.

The youth of today look for amusement, which does not connect with the Saviour, and this leads to misunderstanding.

We must plunge ourselves into the Sacred Heart of Jesus. The world needs to know the infinite joy of the consecration to Jesus's Sacred Heart.

Life can be tough, especially during this present pandemic of the coronavirus.

Corona means crown. Let's crown our lives with a deep devotion to the Sacred Heart. That way, our prayer life begins to have more effect.

These heartfelt prayers bring joy amid suffering.

Jesus is the supernatural Physician. If we get down on our knees, and in true humility ask Him to help us, He will. Open your heart and truly feel the words resonate throughout your soul. Have a true heart-to-heart with the Saviour at this very moment of surrender, and you will begin to see astounding miracles.

Don't give up asking and praying. Too many people turn away from Jesus if they don't get a quick answer. He sometimes tests you like gold in a furnace.

Jesus is looking for commitment to prayer.

I remember being told a true story about a woman who was suffering from cancer. She went to her local chapel, and after Mass, she knelt at the front of the altar and spoke to Jesus saying; "I'm not leaving here until you heal me."

She knelt at that altar for many hours.

She didn't give up.

Finally, after many hours of heartfelt prayer, she felt a surge of heat flow through her whole body. She was healed.

Jesus watched and heard that prayer from the Heart and rewarded her for her diligence and total faith in His Loving Mercy.

Chapter 26
Intimacy With The
Sacred Heart

What does it mean to be intimate with The Sacred Heart? It means to rest our thoughts, our actions, and our way of life – within the beating Heart of Jesus.

To rest, how can we do this?

During this time of the coronavirus pandemic, there is ample time for solitude which enables us to ponder: our relationship with Jesus and to rest in the silence of our hearts listening to the still silent voice of Jesus - pleading with us to come closer to Him.

In the mornings especially, I experience a still voice within me, speaking lovingly to me as I wake up. Jesus tells me to be more intimate, more loving, in my life towards others. That private prompting means we become attuned to the very vibrancy of Jesus's beating Heart within us.

It is a vibrancy that brings solace in these present times of uncertainty in the world.

Oh, if the world could seek solace in Our Lord's Sacred Heart.

Oh, if the world would seriously look at the silent holocaust of abortion.

It seems incredible that through the worldwide Covid-19 lockdown that abortion clinics are now being closed down. How Our Lord must be overjoyed at the closure of these killing factories. I can also imagine huge throngs of angels rejoicing. Our Lord's intimacy will reach out lovingly towards those saved babies.

In the same way, we should be seeking a more intimate life within His most Sacred Heart.

Jesus's Heart is perfect, although His human aspect experiences pain and heartache at the continued sin in the world.

Jesus loves the sinner but hates the sin.

During this time of isolation, I was made aware of three connections between the coronavirus and sin.

Firstly, there is the infection aspect. The Covid-19 virus causes infection, but so does sin. We infect our very souls by sinning.

Secondly, in these present days there is isolation and social distancing. Sin does that too. We become isolated from Jesus when we sin.

And finally, the Covid-19 virus is causing many deaths throughout the world. When we sin, we die ourselves, and more importantly, we distance ourselves from the Sacredness of the Sacred Heart of Jesus.

One thing that has become apparent in the present climate of uncertainty is the rallying call of people in the United Kingdom towards the National Health Service.

There seems to be a certain unity of hearts and willingness to help people who are suffering the effects of the coronavirus isolation. Therefore, we must conclude that even in times of stress, and some people may say, a time of unpleasant spiritual battles – grace abounds.

One area that I haven't touched on is the obvious connection between the Sacred Hearts of Jesus and Mary.

I will explain this in more detail in the next couple of chapters.

Chapter 27
The Twelve Promises of
The Sacred Heart of Jesus

1. I will give them all the graces necessary for their state of life.
2. I will establish peace in their families.
3. I will console them in all their troubles.
4. They shall find in My Heart an assured refuge during life and especially at the hour of death.
5. I will pour abundant blessings on all their undertakings.
6. Sinners shall find in My Heart the source of an infinite ocean of Mercy.
7. Tepid souls shall become fervent.
8. Fervent souls shall speedily rise to great perfection.
9. I will bless the homes where an image of my Heart shall be exposed and honoured.
10. I will give to priests the power of touching the most hardened hearts.
11. Those who propagate this devotion shall have their names written in My Heart.
12. The all-powerful love of My Heart will grant to all those who shall receive Communion on the First Friday of nine consecutive months the grace of final repentance; they shall not die under my displeasure, nor without receiving the Sacraments; My Heart shall be their assured refuge at that last hour.

Chapter 28
The United Hearts of
Jesus and Mary

When we see the blood pouring from Jesus's wounds, it never really occurs to some people that mixed with His sacred blood is the holy blood of His Mother Mary.

Yes, it is a fact that seems to be overlooked.

Our Lady was His mother, therefore, her blood coursed through His veins too.

So, every drop of blood Our Blessed Lord shed on His road to Calvary, was spiritually mixed with the blood of Our Lady. Imagine the scene on the Via Dolorosa, Jesus being beaten and falling three times. His excruciating agony was increased by the violent attacks of the Roman soldiers. He was punched, spat on, rubbish thrown at Him. Horrible insults only served to increase His humiliation. And yet Our Blessed Lord yearned to accomplish the mission of His crucifixion for our sins.

Imagine the trail of blood flowing through the narrow streets of the Via Dolorosa. Jesus's blood mixed with His mother's oozed over the ancient stone pathway, creating a river of mercy for mankind. And yet His mother Mary stayed silent. She could only weep at the horrible sight of her Son being mutilated and abused for our sins.

Our Lord has said previously, "Mankind does not fear God

and sin any longer, but cancer, yes, it is afraid of it – but this is my scourge."

In a touch of irony, sin really *is* a cancer of the soul. Yet people fear cancer more than sin.

Cancer, which begins and grows at the smallest cell in the body, is the same as sin.

The scourge of cancer would be solved if we destroyed sin at its smallest root.

"Mankind cannot research a cure because it does not live in My Will. I would not conceal My secrets from them, but instead the people, in their pride listen to the spirit of evil for this secret begins already, with the smallest imperfection not to live in the Will of God but to enforce one's own pride and wilfulness." (From *The Prayer of Devotion to The United Hearts of Jesus and Mary*)

Yet, in spite of it, God in His love for us, and because of our suffering of atonement, wants to help mankind.

It is a timely reminder for all of us, that the next time we rest our head on a statue of the Sacred Heart of Jesus, we are also simultaneously resting with His mother Mary too.

What a wonderful thought. United in love forever.

The maternal power of Our Blessed Mother is often overlooked too. She has been chosen to crush the serpent with her heel.

No wonder demons flee from her virginal presence.

We should praise God for having such a wonderful heavenly Mother. Any real Mother wants to try and protect her children, and through Our Blessed Mother's maternal intercession, we can be assured of a quick and direct route to Jesus.

When we honour Mary, Jesus pours even more graces upon us, because He sees that act of loving His Mother, as a direct sign of obedience to Him also.

United Hearts of Jesus and Mary, we love You.

Now I feel in my heart, I have come to the end of this short book about the Eternal Sacredness of Our Lord's Sacred Heart.

My only hope is that the words contained in my book may have touched someone's heart in a meaningful way.

I think it would now be appropriate to leave the final words to Saint Margaret Mary Alacoque:

"Love triumphs, Love enjoys, Love finds in God its joys."

Acknowledgements

Special thanks to: my wife, May Livingston, always there in the background; Father Alex Stewart (my Spiritual Director), a gentle guide and spiritual helper; Ellen and James Hrkach, who are always supportive; Tony Fitzpatrick, who is forever inspiring me; Patricia McCarron, who is always an inspiration and to Iain Farry, a faithful friend. Finally, to all family friends and relatives for their support and love throughout the years.

About the Author

Joe is a retired engineer who travels the world extensively. He is now an international speaker.

Joe had a very powerful spiritual conversion in April 1993, which changed his life dramatically. He now travels the world, speaking on behalf of Jesus and His Blessed Mother Mary. His talks have recently centred on the topics of Forgiveness, Reconciliation, and Healing. Joe's work for Our Lord has taken him throughout Europe and more interestingly to Jerusalem in May 2017 where he spoke to a mainly Judaic audience including many rabbis. There were many healings during his talk about Reconciliation, including the rabbi who helped to organise the conference. As a result of the success of this talk, he was invited to speak in Phoenix Arizona in mid-February 2019 by the same organisation C.O.I. (Commonwealth of Israel). Invites to Africa and India are also pending. Here in Scotland, Joe is kept busy at Healing Services, Talks, and Medjugorje evenings with conference invites to England, Wales and Northern Ireland already being planned. Joe was also invited to speak at the Scottish Parliament (Time for Reflection) on Tuesday, March 12, 2019.

The Sacredness of the Sacred Heart is Joe's fourth book.

Joe's first book is entitled *You Are Mine Now*. His second book is a children's fantasy novel called *Oasis of Peace* that was co-written with Tony Fitzpatrick (ex-professional footballer) and released in 2019. Joe's third book is called *The Very Real Dangers of The New Age*, and this is available at his talks.

At the beginning of the Covid-19 lockdown, Joe was prompted by the Holy Spirit to begin a series of talks entitled, "The Clarion Call Talks." For more information, check out his website below.

Joe lives in Glasgow, Scotland with his wife May. His two children Joseph and Anthony are married. Joe and May are now the proud grandparents of six grandchildren. Joe is available for a parish talk, healing service, retreat or conference. You can contact him on 07445 810350. E: joelivingston1967@gmail.com
Website: **www.foundationoftruth.org.uk**

www.ingramcontent.com/pod-product-compliance
Lightning Source LLC
Chambersburg PA
CBHW031323060726
47590CB00003B/1313